The natural world

OXFORD
PRIMARY
art

Norman Binch

Landscape studies

These illustrations are all of studies, or sketches, done in watercolour directly from the landscape.

The first two show us how the artists suggest distance by making the hills very dark.

1

2

1. David Cox (1783-1859). Landscape with sunset, c.1835

2. Peter de Wint. View Clee Hills. c.1840

3. J. M. W. Turner. The sun setting over the sea in an orange mist, c. 1825

4. John Constable (1776-1837). Study of clouds at Hampstead. c.1830

In the others the artists have painted quick studies of moving clouds and sunlight in clouds.

Why not try doing some sketches like this yourself?

3

4

Sea and rivers

1

The seaside, rivers, and waterfalls are favourite subjects for artists.

What are the main differences between these three pictures? Can you see which is the oil painting, which is the watercolour and which is the print?

What is a print?

2

1. James Abbott McNeil Whistler (1834-1903). Nocturne in blue and green, 1871. Tate Gallery

2. Thomas Collier (1840-91). Pensarn Beach, 1886

3. Katsushika Hokusai (1760-1849). The waterfall of Yoshino

3

Gardens

Monet's paintings of water-lilies in his garden at Giverny are famous. Compare the photograph taken in 1992 with the painting done almost a hundred years ago. He experimented with colour and tried to capture impressions of light and the time of day.

1

Can you see any differences between Monet's painting of his garden and the one by Bonnard?

2

3

4

1. A photograph of the view in No. 4, 1992

2. Claude Monet (1840-1926). The Artist's Garden at Vetheuil

3. Pierre Bonnard (1867-1947). The Garden, 1936

4. Claude Monet. White Nenuphars, 1899

More gardens

Artists often choose simple subjects like chairs in a
garden. Why do you think they make paintings of
such subjects?

1

2

Are these two paintings similar in any way?

What do you think they are about?

1. **Anne Jessop. Still life with deck chair and a bowl of fruit**

2. **Valerie Daniel. Summer garden**

3. **Derold Page. Topiary herb garden**

4. **David Inshaw. The badminton game, 1973**

3

4

Tree studies

These watercolour studies of tree trunks show how carefully the artists looked at them and how accurately they recorded what they saw. They would have learnt a lot about trees and how to draw them by this detailed observation.

1

2

3

It would have been helpful to them in making more imaginative paintings of trees, like Samuel Palmer's painting of trees in a garden.

What can you see in this painting?

1. John Downman (1750-1824) A tree trunk near Albano, 1774

2. Joshua Christall (1768-1847). Study of a beech tree stem, 1803

3. Albert Joseph Moore (1841-93). Study of an ash trunk

4. Samuel Palmer (1805-81). In a Shoreham garden

4

Animal and bird studies

These studies of animals and birds were done for the same reasons as the drawings of tree trunks.

Can you think of some of the difficulties the artists might have had in doing detailed drawings of animals and birds? How do you think they might have been done?

Have you tried it yourself? What problems did you have?

2

1

1. J. M. W. Turner. Head of a heron. c. 1815

2. James Ward. Two studies of an eagle, c. 1851

3. Jacques de Gheyn (1565-1629). Studies of field mice

3

Cats

The two studies of cats on this page
are similar to the drawings of birds
and mice, but they are not so detailed.
Can you say how these were done and
with what materials?

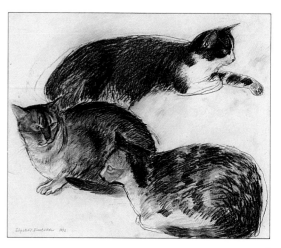

1

2

Can you see what is happening in this Indian painting?

Why do you think the artist Leonard Rosoman painted this picture of his cat? Perhaps because he loves it?

3

4

1. Elizabeth Blackadder. RA. Three cats

2. John Ward. RA. Studies of a cat, 1992

3. Maharaja's tiger shoot. Kotah, Rajasthan. c.1790

4. Leonard Rosoman. RA. Cat with flowers

Natural form

1

Henry Moore has drawn from trees to get ideas for carvings of a mother and child. The mulberry paper flowers cleverly imitate the real thing, and the block print is made of shapes like leaves and buds.

Why do you think the artist painted an onion and an oyster shell?

2

1. William Henry Hunt (1790-1864). An oyster shell and an onion. c. 1859

2. Block printing on handmade paper. Nepal

3. Henry Moore (1898-1986). Tree forms as mother and child, 1950

4. Mulberry paper flowers. North Thailand

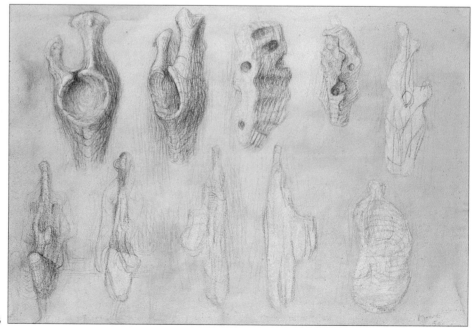

3

16

4

Reeds and grasses

What kind of drawing instruments do you think the artist used to make this study of grasses?

1

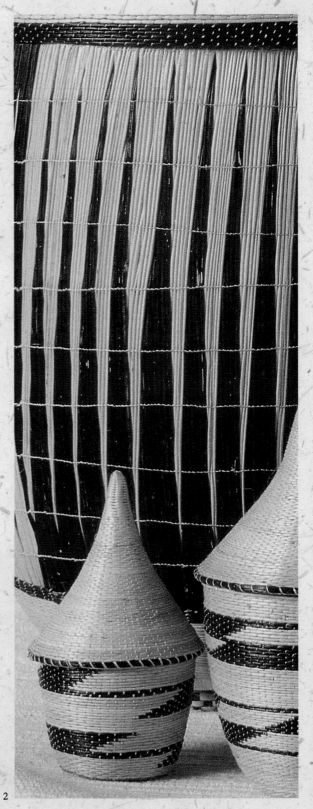

2

1. Albrecht Dürer (1471-1528). Tall grass

2. Zig Zag patterned baskets. Ruanda

3. Basket weaving. Philippines

4. Plaited baskets - detail. North Thailand

Grasses and reeds are used for making baskets. How do you think the patterns are formed? You can try simple weaving using strips of paper or thin card to see how patterns can be made.

3

4

Bulls and cows

The prehistoric cave paintings of bulls and a cow were probably made as a kind of magic to help hunters. Can you imagine what it might have been like to be a painter at that time? Where would you get colours from?

1

2

What does the shape of the plate represent in Picasso's bull decoration?

Elisabeth Frink's two life-sized sculptures of cows are placed in a natural setting. Would they look good in other places, in an art gallery or in town, for instance?

3

1. **Bull with Long Horns, from 15 000 BC Lascaux, France. The Hall of Bulls**

2. **Cave Painting of a Black Cow, 15 000 BC. Lascaux, France**

3. **Pablo Picasso (1881-1973). A bull. (Ceramic plate decoration)**

4. **Elisabeth Frink (1930-93). Two Water Buffaloes**

4

Young animals

These are all sculptures of young animals. Two are carved in stone and one has been modelled in clay, then cast. Can you guess what material Anne Carrington's horse is made from?

Do you know what casting is?

Why do you think the stone carvings are of animals in a curled up position?

1

2

3

4

1. Ann Carrington. Rolling horse and rearing horse, 1992

2. Elizabeth Frink. Rolling horse

3. David McFall. Calf

4. John Skeaping. Stone sculpture of a dachsund, 1933

Horses

1

The two paintings are of horses which have been frightened by lightning. The one by Delacroix is dramatic and the horse is clearly very frightened. Can you say how Géricault has shown the horse's fear?

The bronze horse is a memorial to a horse called Hyperion. The Chinese horse was placed in the tomb of an important person for use in his life after death.

2

3

1. Eugène Delacroix (1798-1863). Rearing horse frightened by lightning

2. Théodore Géricault (1791-1824). A horse frightened by lightning

3. John Skeaping. Hyperion, 1961

4. Chinese tomb figure. Tang Dynasty, 700-750 AD

4

Elephants and tigers

In Asia, elephants have been used for work since early times. They were also ridden in processions and for hunting tigers, when they would be highly decorated.

Can you see how the decorations were made in these two paintings?

1

2

Henri Rousseau is famous for his paintings of the jungle and of tigers. In fact he never went to a jungle but worked in his own garden and used his imagination to paint scenes like these.

Animals' markings, like a tiger's stripes, act as camouflage in the jungle.

How many different kinds of plants and trees can you see?

1. Indian painting on cotton of a tiger hunt

2. Indian painting on silk of an elephant

3. Henri Rousseau (1875-1933). Tropical storm with a tiger, 1891

4. Henri Rousseau. Tropical forest - battling tiger and bull, 1908

Decoration

These are more examples of artists using nature for their ideas.

Can you identify the animals?

The gold brooches were made by modelling the animals in wax or clay and then taking casts from a mould. A mould is made from the model and then filled with molten gold – like using a jelly mould.

Bernard Leach was influenced by potters from the Far East. You have a go at painting a fish in as few strokes of the brush as you can.

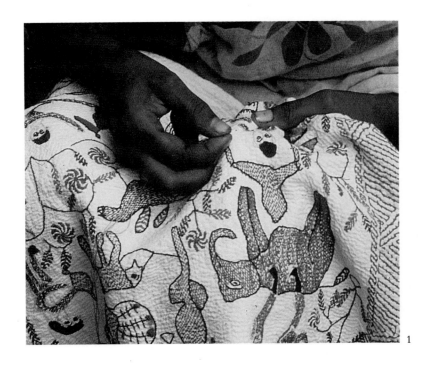

1

2

3

1. Embroidered decoration.
Kantha, India

2. Selection of gold animal
brooches

3. Bernard leach, (1887-1979).
Leaping fish vase, 1960

Things to do

Try to find some landscape or seascape views and make some studies like the ones on pages 2 and 3. Use materials such as watercolours, inks, and pastels, and try using them together sometimes.

From your studies make some paintings at home.

Do some careful, detailed drawings of trees, plants, animals, and birds to get information. Try to understand their structure - how they grow or move.

From your studies, use your imagination to make pictures
or models of exciting and dramatic events.

Words to remember

block printing – printing from the surface of a piece of wood, lino, a potato or other suitable things to create patterns.

casting – making a mould from a model then filling it with another material, such as plaster, bronze, gold etc. to get an exact copy of the original – like using a jelly mould.

detailed observation – looking very carefully at things and making drawings which accurately record what you see and understand.

sketches – similar to studies but usually less detailed and done freely and quickly

structure – the way something is constructed – how a building is put together – how a plant or tree grows – how its shape is formed by the trunk, branches and stems – the framework or skeleton of something.

studies – drawings or sketches of things or people which are made to get information or to try out an idea before making the final object.

The publishers would like to thank the following for permission to reproduce photographs and other copyright material :

pp 2/3 1 *Private Collection;* **2** *Private Collection;* **3** *Victoria and Albert Museum;* **4** *Tate Gallery;* **pp 4/5 1** *Tate Gallery;* **2** *Fitzwilliam Museum, Cambridge;* **3** *Bridgeman Art Library Private Collection;* **pp 6/7 1** *The author;* **2** *Bridgeman Art Library/National Gallery of Art, Washington;* **3** *Bridgeman Art Library/Musee du Petit Palais, Paris © ADAGP/SPADEM, Paris and DACS, London 1994;* **4** *Bridgeman Art Library/Pushkin Museum, Moscow;* **pp 8/9 1** *Bridgeman Art Library/John Noott Galleries, Broadway, Worcs;* **2** *Bridgeman Art Library/Private Collection;* **3** *Bridgeman Art Library/Private Collection;* **4** *Tate Gallery;* **pp 10/11 1** *Private Collection;* **2** *British Museum;* **3** *Ashmolean Museum, Oxford;* **4** *Bridgeman Art Library/Victora and Albert Museum, London;* **pp 12/13 1** *Leeds City Art Galleries;* **2** *Fitzwilliam Museum, Cambridge;* **pp 14/15 1** *Royal Academy of Arts/© The artist;* **2** *Royal Academy of Arts/© The artist;* **3** *Victoria and Albert Museum;* **pp 16/17 1** *Private Collection;* **2** *Oxfam/Emma Gough;* **3** *Bridgeman Art Library/Private Collection © The Henry Moore Foundation;* **4** *Oxfam/Letts;* **pp 18/19 2** *Oxfam/Letts;* **3** *Oxfam/Peter McCulloch;* **4** *Oxfam/Letts;* **pp 20/21 1** *Bridgeman Art Library/Caves of Lascaux, France;* **2** *Bridgeman Art Library/Caves of Lascaux, France;* **3** *Bridgeman Art Library/Bonhams, London © DACS 1994;* **4** *Bridgeman Art Library/Private Collection;* **pp 22/23 1** *The artist;* **2** *Bridgeman Art Library/Private Collection;* **3** *Tate Gallery/Bowes Museum, Barnard Castle;* **4** *Bridgeman Art Library/ The Fine Art Society, London;* **pp 24/25 2** *National Gallery;* **3** *Bridgeman Art Library/Stanley House Collection, Newmarket;* **4** *Victoria and Albert Museum;* **pp 26/27 1** *Bridgeman Art Library/Private Collection;* **2** *Bridgeman Art Library;* **3** *Bridgeman Art Library/National Gallery, London;* **4** *Bridgeman Art Library/ Hermitage, St Petersburg;* **pp 28/29 1** *Oxfam/Badal;* **2** *Bridgeman Art Library/Bonhams, London;* **3** *Crafts Council*

We would also like to thank **Jeff Tearle** and the pupils of **Frideswide Middle School, Oxford**, and **Michael Mayell** and pupils of **St. Philip and St. James First School, Oxford**, for help with the Things To Do Sections. The photography in the Things To Do Sections was by **Martin Sookias and Mike Dudley.**

Oxford University Press, Walton Street, Oxford OX2 6DP
© Oxford University Press